Generous Loving, Generous Giving

WALT RUSSELL

RECLAIMED
PUBLISHING

Generous Loving, Generous Giving
© 2013 Walt Russell

Published by Reclaimed Publishing
a division of Reclaimed, Inc.
reclaimedpublishing@gmail.com

Unless otherwise identified, all Scripture
quotations in this publication are taken from the
New American Standard Bible (NASB), © The
Lockman Foundation. Other Scripture quotations
are taken from The Holy Bible, English Standard
Version © 2001 by Crossway Bibles, a division of
Good New Publishers. Used by permission. All
rights reserved. All emphases in Scripture
quotations have been added by the author.

Cover design by John-Mark Warkentin
www.jmwarkentin.com

ISBN 13: 978-0615939070
ISBN 10: 0615939074

I am grateful to Wes Willmer for his great understanding, kindness, and feedback in the writing of this book.

CONTENTS

INTRODUCTION

Many evangelicals approach the subject of biblical giving as if they were bracing for a financial root canal. It goes like this: "Oh, I know I need to be more unselfish and spend less on myself and give more back to God. But it's such a painful process!" The assumption is that the core motivation for biblical giving is *self-denial*. More to God, less to me. However, when we examine the Old and New Testaments, we do not find that *self-denial* is the driving force behind giving. Quite the contrary.

C. S. Lewis noted this faulty motivation not just about giving, but about the entire Christian life in his marvelous essay, "The Weight of Glory." Lewis makes this telling observation:

"If you asked twenty good men to-day what they thought the highest of the virtues, nineteen of them would reply, *Unselfishness*. But if you asked almost any of the great Christians of old he would have replied, *Love*. You see what has happened? A negative term has been substituted for a positive, and this is of more than philological importance. The negative ideal of *Unselfishness* carries with it the suggestion not primarily of securing good things for others, but of going without them ourselves, *as if our abstinence and not their happiness was the important point.* I do not think this is the Christian virtue of *Love*."[1]

It seems that the substitution of the

---

[1] "The Weight of Glory," in *The Weight of Glory and Other Addresses* (Wm. B. Eerdmans, 1949) 1; italics are mine.

negative term *Unselfishness* has also triumphed quite grandly over the positive virtue of *Love* in many of our discussions about biblical giving. We fall into the narcissistic modern pattern of assuming that *our self-denial* is the primary point. Again, Lewis challenges our misplaced emphasis:

"The New Testament has lots to say about *self-denial*, but not about self-denial as an end in itself. We are told to deny ourselves and to take up our crosses in order that we may follow Christ; and nearly every description of what we shall ultimately find if we do so contains an appeal to *desire*. If there lurks in most modern minds the notion that to desire our own good and earnestly to hope for the enjoyment of it is a bad thing, I submit that this notion has crept in from Kant and the Stoics and is no part of the Christian faith. Indeed, if we consider the unblushing promises of reward and the staggering nature of the rewards promised in the Gospels, it would seem that Our Lord finds our desires, not too strong, but too weak. We are half-hearted creatures, fooling about with drink and sex and ambition when infinite joy is offered us, like an ignorant child who wants to go on making mud pies in a slum because he cannot imagine what is meant by the offer of a holiday at the sea. We are far too easily pleased."[2]

The thesis of this book is that the Bible's emphasis on giving is rooted in an appeal to at least three of our most fundamental desires: our desire to love God in response to His love of us, our desire to love others, and our desire to be seen and rewarded by God when we stand before Him. While such giving includes the negative aspect of self-denial at certain points, self-denial is not the core of the biblical motivation. Rather, the Bible records God's attempts to appeal to our desires to love others in response to His lavish love of us in Christ. To learn to give generously,

---

[2] "The Weight of Glory," 1-2; italics are mine.

therefore, is not to learn to deny self vigorously, but to learn to love generously as we are so loved. Giving generously is about loving generously.

Some Unloving Giving Statistics

It would appear that we have much to learn about loving generously by giving generously. As has been well documented over a broad range of surveys, the average percentage Evangelical Christians in the United States now give is between 2 and 3% of their gross income.[3] Such a figure is so shocking to some Christians that their displeasure has spilled over into the modern theological forum—the bumper sticker. Here's a recent one I saw in Southern California: "If you love Jesus, tithe. Anyone

---

[3] For a broad, ecumenical perspective on the giving crisis in the church in America, see Mark Chaves and Sharon L. Miller, eds., *Financing American Religion* (Walnut Creek, CA: Alta Mira Press, 1999), especially Chapter 8, "The Crisis in the Churches," by Robert Wuthnow, 67-76.

can honk." I appreciate the heartfelt reaction to superficial Christianity. I also appreciate the linking of loving Jesus by loving others with our giving. What is so amazing about the Bible is that it records how God has gone to great lengths to teach His children this very thing. This is a thread that runs throughout the Old Testament and into the New.

WHY DOES GOD WANT US TO GIVE GENEROUSLY?

The short answer is that generous giving has astonishing effects. God wants us to give because of the effects that are caused by our generosity. In His kindness God has given us several perspectives on what these effects will be. The following are four of the New Testament pictures of the eternal effects from generous causes.

Sowing and Reaping Generously

The Old Testament previously connected the sowing and reaping of grain to giving (Psalm 112:9; Proverbs 11:24-16; 22:9). However, the fullest development of this concept is left to Paul in 2 Corinthians 9:6-15. The broader context in 2 Corinthians 8-9 is the exhortation to the Corinthians to complete the collection for the impoverished churches of Jerusalem and Judea.[4] Among Paul's many encouragements to the Corinthian believers in these chapters is the motivational principle that God will reward with a spiritual harvest in direct proportion to generous sowing/giving. Paul develops this concept in 2 Corinthians 9:6-15:

1. <u>The Principle</u> (v. 6) – The one who sows sparingly shall also reap

---

[4] See Ben Witherington III, *Conflict & Community in Corinth: A Socio-Rhetorical Commentary on 1 and 2 Corinthians* (Grand Rapids, MI: William B. Eerdmans Publishing Company, 1995) 411-423 for a culturally-sensitive treatment of this collection.

sparingly; the one who sows bountifully shall also reap bountifully.

2. <u>The Individual's Choice</u> (v. 7) – "Let each one do just as he has purposed in his heart; not grudgingly or under compulsion; for God loves a cheerful giver."

3. <u>God's Generous Provision of Our Seed for Sowing</u> (vv. 8-11)

(vv. 8-9) – We'll have all sufficiency and abundance for every good deed and our righteousness will abide forever.

(vv. 10-11) – We'll never lack seed to sow generously because God will supply and multiply our resources so that we'll never lack the ability to give liberally![5]

4. <u>The Impact of Our Generous Sowing/Giving</u> (vv. 12-15)

Our giving will fully supply the needs of the saints (12a).

Our giving will also stir people to give thanks to God because of our obedience and generosity (12b-13).

Our giving will also cause people to pray for us and yearn for us (14-15).

Notice that 80% of Paul's argument focuses on the motivational aspects of the giving. Eight of the ten

---

[5] John Chrysostom (died 407) says, "If God rewards those who till the earth with abundance, how much more will he reward those who till the soil of heaven in caring for the soul?" *Homilies on the Epistles of Paul to the Corinthians* 20.1 (Ancient Christian Commentary on Scripture, New Testament VII: 1-2 Corinthians , Gerald Bray, ed.; Downers Grove, IL: InterVarsity Press, 1999) 281.

verses deal with God's gracious provision for our needs if we give generously (vv. 8-11) and with the astonishing impact of our giving (vv. 12-15). This is not a heavy-handed obligatory appeal, but rather an attempt to motivate believers to choose to give generously to their fellow believers and churches. It is an appeal to our desire! Within the freedom not to give, God motivates us to choose to give by appealing to our desire. The filter that separates good motives from bad is that of cheerfulness (v. 7b). If a spirit of freedom and cheerfulness does not accompany our giving, then we need to check our motives. No freedom; no cheerfulness; keep your money! That's an astonishing part of the beauty of New Covenant grace-giving. Grudging compulsion should give way pretty quickly to cheerful choosing.

I have tested the concepts in these verses and found them to be amazingly encouraging. For example, just three weeks ago I was walking back to my office on campus at Biola University when an international student intersected my path and said that he needed to talk to me. He wanted to apologize for getting a bad grade in one of my graduate courses the previous semester! As we approached my office door, I saw an envelope in the book on the door and absent-mindedly picked it up and threw it on my desk as we entered the office. We sat down to talk about his situation.

The short story was that last semester was his second in the United States and his children had been ill, his wife had been depressed, and he had been working long hours to pay the doctor bills while taking a full load of graduate courses in a second language. No wonder he had been unable to complete the work in my course! I was so touched by his tender heart and difficult circumstances that I began to weep along with him. After we both cried for a while, he asked me to pray for him. I tried to collect myself emotionally, put my hand on his shoulder, and began to pray.

Within ten seconds of beginning my prayer I heard a voice in my mind—which I immediately sensed as the Lord's—and the voice said, "Empty your wallet!" Now this sort of thing doesn't happen to me every day! In fact, it was so straightforward and unusual that I was taken aback and didn't even try to quibble with the Lord. I just quickly finished my prayer, took out my wallet, opened it and gave this dear brother the contents. I told him I wished it was more, but it was all that I had at the time. However, I told him that the Lord wanted him and his dear family to know that the Lord saw their need and loved them very much. He looked at the crumpled bills in his lap and said with tears coming down his cheeks that it was like receiving a million dollars.

After a few more tears, we parted company. As I was again trying to collect myself emotionally, I picked up the envelope that had been in my door-box. Inside it was an anonymous letter from a graduate student in one of classes. The student noted that I had bought a small book for each person in the class (because I had forgotten to put it on the course booklist) and that several students had forgotten to repay me for my expenditure. Concerned that I would suffer a financial loss in the deal, the student gave me several twenty dollar bills. Immediately I knew that this anonymous brother or sister's generosity was directly connected to my choosing to empty my wallet two or three minutes earlier! I had to sit down in my chair and weep because of the wonderful faith-stretching and encouraging experience that my Heavenly Father had just constructed for me. The money in the envelope was more than double what I had just given the international student. The promise about generous, cheerful giving was again etched in the deep recesses of my soul: "Now He who supplies seed to the sower and bread for food, will supply and multiply your seed for sowing...." (2 Corinthians 9:10).[6]

I can attest that God has been faithful beyond measure to supply plenty of seed to sow when I have sown it abundantly during my forty-nine years as a Christian. God's creativity in supplying the seed is seemingly endless. He has stirred the hearts of His people to put money in my Bible at church, or cash in an envelope on my doorstep (or door-box!), or anonymous money orders in the mail, or many, many unexpected checks in the mail from

---

[6] This story continues in a marvelous manner. A few days after this incident, I shared this international student's story at a church retreat in my talk on generous giving. God stirred the hearts of a young couple to give of their abundance to meet the needs of financially-struggling students at our school. This couple just emailed me a few moments ago and they committed to support this international student and his family $1000/month! God is amazingly gracious and kind in allowing us to be a part of what He is doing in the world. We simply sow the seed that He ever so generously supplies!

Christian family members. But God has also used insurance companies and surprising refunds, random rebates on products, additional funds from the selling of some asset, and especially, some lucrative additional work that He clearly provided for me. In light of my experience, my exhortation to you is *to sow generously*! Our Heavenly Father has said that He "will supply and multiply your seed for sowing. ....and you will be enriched in everything for all liberality" (vv. 10-11). And you will.

Laying Up Treasures in Heaven

This motivation interpenetrates all other aspects of giving. It is a crucial piece for our motivational mosaic. We will encounter this concept in Luke 16:9-13 in the parable of the unjust manager. There, Jesus speaks of heavenly rewards by speaking of our "friends" welcoming us into our eternal dwellings (v. 9), God's entrusting of "true riches" to us (v. 11), and His giving to us "that which is our own" (v. 12).

Paul appeals to these same concepts in 1 Timothy 6:17-19

Instruct those who are rich in this present world not to be conceited or to fix their hope on the uncertainty of riches, but on God, who richly supplies us with all things to enjoy. Instruct them to do good, to be rich in good works, to be generous and ready to share, storing up for themselves the treasure of a good foundation for the future, so that they may take hold of that which is life indeed.

Note Paul's numerous word-plays in these verses.[7] The rich are only rich in this present world (lit. *age*) and should be preparing for the future, i.e., the age-to-come. Their focus should not be on their riches, which are uncertain, but on *being rich in good works*. This will give them a wonderful *heavenly treasure*, which gets their

---

[7] See William D. Mounce, *Word Biblical Commentary: Pastoral Epistles* (Nashville, TN: Thomas Nelson Publishers, 2000) 365-369,

hands on that which is life indeed, *their heavenly treasure and home*. Rightly understanding how life extends eternally into the future gives the rich the right perspective in the here and now. This is truly tapping into *an eternal desire*.

Perhaps the best-known and most memorable words about laying up treasures in heaven are Jesus' words in Matthew 6:19-21:

> Do not lay up for yourselves treasures upon earth, where moth and rust destroy, and where thieves break in and steal. But lay up for yourselves treasures in heaven, where neither moth nor rust destroys, and where thieves do not break in or steal; for where your treasure is, there will your heart be also.

Certainly these are beautiful and comforting words which God has destined us to experience.[8] But Jesus also challenges

---

[8] For a brief and motivating discussion of believers' eternal rewards, see the stimulating book by Randy Alcorn, *Money, Possessions & Eternity* (Wheaton, IL: Tyndale House Publishers, Inc., 1989), especially 153-169.

us to keep a proper focus on our heavenly home. Linked to the seductive power and serving of riches (instead of God) is the corresponding focus on creating earthly wealth and security (rather than heavenly wealth). As both Jesus and Paul assert, such a focus is wrapped with *uncertainty* due to the multiple threats to such wealth. God loves us too much to allow us to build our lives on flimsy stuff that will fail, that is a very little thing, that is not true riches, and that actually belongs to another (Luke 16:9-13). The only path out of such a maze is to set our heart and focus upon our heavenly home and our heavenly treasure.

The best way to have such a heart-focus is to spend our way there! In other words we should be investing our treasure in those people and things that will make a difference in heaven. As our treasure is flowing in a heavenward direction, then our hearts will follow along behind it. This is the point of Jesus' words, "for where your treasure is, there will your heart be also" (Matthew 6:21). This means that choosing to give back to the Lord a portion of what He has given us will actually help us keep our hearts focused on that which really matters and that which is life indeed. This is why generous giving is so very central to our growth in Christ. While our heart usually initiates our giving, the converse can also true. Our giving can reshape our heart and our heart-focus.[9] This is simply another amazing aspect of grace-giving and the Bible's appeal to our desire to love generously by giving generously.

---

[9] Jesus' words to the church in Ephesus in Revelation 2:4-5a underscore that our hearts can be remolded by our deeds or actions:

> But I have this against you, that you have left your first love. Remember therefore from where you have fallen, and repent and *do the deeds you did at first*;

Doing the actions that the Ephesians did when they first believed would help remold their heart-affections to that which they had as new believers. This is also, in part, the purpose of the spiritual disciplines. See especially Dallas Willard, *The Spirit of the Disciplines: Understanding How God Changes Lives* (San Francisco, CA: Harper & Row, Publishers, 1988).

Making Friends for Eternity

It is unfortunate that the Parable of the Unjust Manager in Luke 16:1-13 is considered to be the most difficult of Jesus' parables to interpret. This is because Jesus chooses a dishonest steward or manager as the main character of the story in Luke 16:1-8. This has vexed commentators and they have gone to great lengths to try and rescue Jesus. However, the quick and straightforward solution is that Jesus is simply focusing on one admirable quality that the dishonest manager possesses. The rest of his actions are corrupt, but he has one significant quality that Christians should seek to emulate. This is what we call an argument from a lesser to a greater. If something is true in its lesser state, then you can be very certain that it will be true in its greater state. If this quality is admirable and expedient in the life of a reprobate, imagine what it will be like in the life of a regenerate person. This is Jesus' basic strategy.[10]

The parable itself is pretty straightforward in Luke 16:1-8. A wealthy man owns a large wholesale agricultural products company. His chief administrator has been found to be dishonest and has been squandering the rich owner's money. The owner tells the manager that he is going to fire him. Now the dishonest guy is in a quandary. He knows that he's going to lose his cushy management job. So, he strategizes:

I'm too weak to dig and too proud to beg. So, I'll make friends with my owner's debt-ridden retailers by significantly reducing their debts. Then, when my time of stewardship is over, they'll welcome me into their homes!

This bill-reduction is exactly what the manager does in verses 5-7. The numbers are astronomical to make the point of the

---

[10] See Robert H. Stein, *The New American Commentary: Luke* (Nashville, TN: Broadman Press, 1992) 410-417 for a concise, yet thorough sifting of the interpretive options and agreement with this book's interpretation.

enormity of their debt and the extravagance of his forgiveness of large portions of the debt. Luke 16:8 closes the parable itself and pivots into Jesus' interpretation of it and His comments about the nature of money:

"And his master praised the unrighteous steward *because he had acted shrewdly*; for the sons of this age are *more shrewd* in relation to their own kind than the sons of light."

This parable is one of the most powerful and insightful teachings about money and giving in the whole Bible! This is so because Jesus' main point in the parable is that *Christians should be as shrewd in using money as non-Christians are*. The sons and daughters of light should know how to use money as skillfully in establishing relationships as the sons and daughters of this age. This is Jesus' main point in Luke 16:9:

"And I say to you, make friends for yourselves by means of the mammon [riches] of unrighteousness; that when it fails, they may receive you into the eternal dwellings."

Lest you miss the astonishing significance of Jesus' point, it is this. We Christians should use our money in such shrewd ways that when our stewardship of it ends (upon our death), then we will have invested in a myriad of "friends" who will welcome us into our heavenly home. In other words we should shrewdly use the privilege of grace-giving to invest in the salvation, spiritual growth, and loving life-development of as many people around the world as we possibly can. In so doing, we are not *spending* money, but rather *investing* it. We are investing it in advancing the gospel cause and thereby are making countless friends who will recognize us as friends throughout eternity! Isn't that an astonishing concept?

In developing His point of using *earthly finances to make eternal friends*, Jesus also underscores these five facts about money:

1. Money will ultimately fail, not if, but when (v. 9).

2. Money is "a very little thing" (v. 10).

3. Money is not the true riches, but God gives us those later if we are faithful (v. 11).

4. Money, which belongs to another, is simply to test our faithfulness as a manager so that God can ultimately reward us with our own (v. 12).

5. Money is also a test to see if we will serve God only and not riches (v. 13).

A few years ago when our family lived in Arlington, Texas, I decided to hire a young neighbor named Arlan to mow our lawn. I was very busy that summer and availed myself of the luxury of his services. The problem was that he didn't do a very good job of mowing around the bushes in the yard the first two times he mowed. I dutifully called him over after each mowing and demonstrated how to get closer to the bushes so he didn't leave a circle of tall grass around every one of them. Each time He shook his head that he understood. However, after his third mowing, we had the same problem.

My solution was simple: fire thirteen-year-old Arlan so that he learned about the harsh realities of the marketplace! Fortunately, my wife Marty intervened and appealed to Luke 16:1-13 and the concept of using earthly finances to make eternal friends. She said that she had been talking to Arlan each week when she gave him a glass of cold water. She said that she had been able to introduce the subject of a personal relationship with Jesus Christ and needed more time to talk with him over the rest of the grass-mowing season. How could I object to the wisdom of Jesus and my wife about the shrewd use of money?

Against, my own instincts I did not fire Arlan and he trusted Christ with Marty within the next two weeks. As I look back on the experience, I'm amazed at the insignificance of a lawn of a house that we no longer own compared to an eternal being entering into a relationship with the Living God. Perhaps those few dollars that I paid Arlan to mow our yard so sloppily were the best investment that I've ever made! I look forward to reconnecting with him when we enter our eternal home.

The bottom line is that Christians march to the beat of a different financial drum when it comes to "investing". We should be investing in cultivating relationships so that only heaven will reveal the shrewdness of our strategy. However, because we know the eternal value of human beings, we know that there is no greater investment. We can now wisely cultivate eternal friendships from all over the world by the shrewd use of our earthly finances. The future desire for eternal friends should motivate us to be generous with present finances. Again, God gives us a picture of the end in order to appeal to our desire in the present.

Putting God and Money in Their Places

In various passages of Scripture, money is viewed as a power or false god demanding our service. Our challenge is to choose to serve God and to put money in its place relative to Him. Jesus said,

"No one can serve two masters; for either he will hate the one and love the other, or he will hold to one and despise the other. You cannot serve God and mammon [riches]" (Matthew 6:24/Luke 16:13).

Jesus' point in these two passages is that serving money or riches cannot occur *alongside* serving God. This is because both money and God make exclusive demands as a master/owner upon their servant. There can be no side-by-side servanthood of both. God rightly and justly demands the supreme role as our Master; money usurps God's role and mimics His demands.[11] When money's and God's demands conflict, we must choose God's. There is no easy or polite way to soften Jesus' words on this matter. They are what they are.[12]

While we may understand Jesus' challenge to us, we may not take it to its logical conclusion. This is where the topic of giving comes to the forefront. Note that Jesus said that a person "will hate the one and love the other, or he will hold to one and despise the other." How can we hold to and love God while simultaneously despising and hating money as a false god? In answer to our question, Jacques Ellul suggests the concept of *profanation*:

To profane money, like all other

---

[11] See Michael J. Wilkins, *The NIV Application Commentary: Matthew* (Grand Rapids, MI: Zondervan, 2004) 295-296 for an insightful discussion of this verse.

[12] For an insightful discussion of this challenge, see R. Scott Rodin, *Stewards of the Kingdom: A Theology of Life in All Its Fullness* (Downers Grove, IL: InterVarsity Press, 2000), especially Chapter 6, "The Myth of the Two Kingdoms," 122-151.

powers, is to take away its sacred character. For although we usually think of profaning goods or values that are religious in a positive sense, it is just as possible to conduct such an assault against Satan and all he inspires…

This profanation, then, means uprooting the sacred character, destroying the element of power. We must bring money back to its simple role as a material instrument. When money is no more than an object, when it has lost its seductiveness, its supreme value, its superhuman splendor, then we can use it like any other of our belongings, like any machine…

Now this profanation is first of all the result of a spiritual battle, but this must be translated into behavior. There is one act par excellence which profanes money by going directly against the law of money, an act for which money is not made. This is *giving*.[13]

The best way to put money in its place is to give the money back to God through any of the various expressions of grace-giving. Giving is perhaps the best means of expressing that God is our Master and that money is not. Giving helps us keep both God and money in their respective places.

An Answer

Perhaps we can now answer our question, "Why does God want us to give generously?" The simple answer is that such generosity will transform both our earthly life and our eternal life.

In the present, we will have an abundance for every good deed, will never lack resources to give generously, and will produce thanksgivings to God by meeting the needs

---

[13] Jacques Ellul, *Money & Power*, English translation of 1979 French edition by LaVonne Neff (Downers Grove, IL: InterVarsity Press, 1984) 109-110.

of the saints (2 Cor 9:8, 11-12). Our generosity will also stir people to give thanks to God and to pray and yearn for us (2 Cor 9:12b-14). Our heart will have a heavenly focus because of our earthly generosity (Matt 6:20). Additionally, we will showcase that we serve God and not riches through our generous giving and that we can be faithful in using money, which is "a very little thing" (Luke 16:12-13; Matt 6:24).

In our resurrected bodies, we will possess a righteousness that abides forever and an increasing harvest of righteousness that God causes (2 Cor 9:9-10). Our generosity will also store up treasures in heaven for us and help us lay hold of that which is life indeed (1 Tim 6:18-19; Matt 6:20). Generous giving today will also result in God giving us "the true riches" (probably kingdom and eternal rewards), which will be our own (Luke 16:12-13). Moreover, we will be making friends for eternity with our shrewd, present investing in people-ministry and the recipients will welcome us into our heavenly home (Luke 16:9).

Because of the transforming effects that our generosity brings, God lovingly reveals glimpses of its earthly and eternal magnitude. Of the latter, C. S. Lewis again brings great clarity to what awaits us:

"The promises of Scripture may very roughly be reduced to five heads. It is promised,

firstly, that we shall be with Christ;

secondly, that we shall be like Him;

thirdly, with an enormous wealth of imagery, that we shall have "glory";

fourthly, that we shall, in some sense, be fed or feasted or entertained; and

finally, that we shall have some sort of official position in the universe—ruling cities, judging angels, being pillars of God's temple."[14]

---

[14] "The Weight of Glory," 7. Believers ruling over cities (or the nations) is discussed in Rev 2:26-27, our judging of angels is in 1 Cor 6:1-3; and our being pillars of God's temple is in Rev 3:12.

The effects of loving through present generous giving will be majestically manifested in the future with heavenly glory, celebration, and rulership in Christ's kingdom and eternity.[15] Of such things we have far too little desire! We are willing to settle for terrestrial mud pies in the slums rather than celestial vacations by the sea.

---

[15] There is a great need among believers to understand what awaits us at our death, at our resurrection, at the return of Christ, and at the advent of the new heavens and the new earth. Perhaps the most accessible recent book on these matters is Randy Alcorn's, *Heaven* (Carol Stream, IL: Tyndale House Publishers, Inc., 2004). An older work but still timely is René Pache, *The Future Life* (Chicago, IL: Moody Press, 1971). For a powerful allegorical tale of heaven and hell (from a biblical perspective), see C. S. Lewis, *The Great Divorce* (HarperSan Francisco; new edition, 2001).

IS GENEROUS GIVING DEFINED BY A PERCENTAGE?

If our generous giving has astonishing effects, both presently and eternally, it would seem that God would want to encourage His children to partake richly of its benefits. This is exactly the story of God's fatherly teaching about giving in the Bible. As we would expect with a nation that grows out of one man's family, it all begins with Father Abram in the Old Testament.

The beginning of generous giving in the Bible is in a somewhat unusual incident in

Genesis 14. After Abram saved Lot, his family and servants, and all his possessions, Abram met with the king of Sodom and the mysterious Melchizedek, the king of Salem, who brought out bread and wine for Abram. The Bible says:

"Now he [Melchizedek] was a priest of God Most High. And he blessed him [Abram] and said,

"Blessed be Abram of God Most High, Possessor of heaven and earth;

And blessed be God Most High, Who has delivered your enemies into your hand.

And he [Abram] gave him a tenth of all" (Genesis 14:18-20).

Since Genesis means "beginnings," we see several beginnings for Israel here:

1. *Tithing in Israel* begins with Father Abram giving a tithe (1/10) to the Lord.
2. *Giving tithes to God's representatives* begins again with Father

Abram giving to a priest—a representative of the Most High God (later the Levites in Israel).

3. *The pattern of giving "first fruits" to the Lord* begins once more with Father Abram giving to the Lord as an immediate recognition of God's provision and grace by giving back to Him right after the "harvest" came in.[16]

4. *The pattern of trusting God and not our neighbors to make us great* begins when Father Abram receives God's blessing from

---

[16] Israel was to give of the first-fruits of the crops of the land, the fruit of the trees, and of her herds and flocks (Exodus 23:14-17; 34:22; Numbers 15:17-21; 18:12; Deuteronomy 18:4). Even King Solomon commented on this and exhorted about giving the first-fruits in Proverbs 3:9-10:

"Honor the Lord from your wealth, and from the first of all your produce;
So your barns will be filled with plenty, and your vats will overflow with new wine."

Melchizedek (Genesis 14:18-20), but refuses the offer from the King of Sodom to keep the captured goods (14:21-24).

Abram's tithing to Melchizedek in Genesis 14:20 establishes the historical foundation of tithing within the Mosaic Covenant. The Mosaic Law simply develops in covenantal format the tithing principles established by Father Abram. As something begins, so it shall continue. The founder establishes its trajectory and pattern.

Before going further into the Old Testament's pattern of giving, it is necessary to jump to a New Testament passage that gives us a developmental framework for interpreting the Old and New Covenants together. Paul views Old Covenant believers collectively as a child, a minor, who is under the tutelage of the Mosaic Law until the time set by the Father:

"Now I say as long as the heir is a child, he does not differ at all from a slave although he is owner of everything, but he is under guardians and managers until the date set by the father. So also we, while we were children, were held in bondage under the elemental things of the world" (Gal 4:1-3)

God our Father set the coming of Jesus the Messiah as "the fullness of time" when God's children passed into the developmental era of adulthood. The passage continues

"But when the fullness of the time came, God sent forth His Son, born of a woman, born under the Law, in order that He might redeem those who were under the Law, that we might receive the adoption as sons. And because you are sons, God has sent forth the Spirit of His Son into our hearts, crying, 'Abba, Father!' Therefore, you are no longer a slave, but a son; and if a son, then an heir through God" (Gal 4:4-7).

It is immensely important to note that this is an appeal to what we now call *stages of moral development*[17] or, even better, *stages of faith development.*[18] Paul's basic appeal is to persuade his readers to enjoy the freedom that comes from being developmentally-adult children under the covenantal maturity of the Messianic age, i.e., the New Covenant. What is left behind is the developmental immaturity when God's children were minors under the Mosaic Law (Gal 3:23-26). Their time of childhood was characterized by the tutelage of the Law Covenant. Their time as adults is now to be characterized by the

---

[17] For example, well-known theorist, Lawrence Kohlberg, identifies six stages of moral development in a person's life. See his book, *Essays on Moral Development, Vol. I: The Philosophy of Moral Development* (San Francisco, CA: Harper & Row, 1981).

[18] See James W. Fowler, *Stages of Faith: The Psychology of Human Development and the Quest for Meaning* (San Francisco, CA: HarperSan Francisco, 1995 paperback; 1981 original). More recently, see Janet O. Hagberg and Robert A. Guelich, *The Critical Journey: Stages in the Life of Faith*, Second Edition (Salem, WI: Sheffield Publishing Company, 2005).

indwelling of the Holy Spirit (Gal 4:6).

This developmental shift is of great significance to the change in God's emphasis on generous giving from the Old to the New Testament. What does *not* change is the importance of giving generously. What *does* change is the amount of structure and percentages surrounding the giving from when God viewed His children as minors. In adulthood many of the guidelines of childhood disappear.

Tithing: The Old Testament Pattern for Generous Giving When God's People Were Minors

It is nevertheless instructive to see how God taught generous giving to His minor-age children. God designed Israel to be a theocratic state, over whom He Himself reigned as the Theocratic Ruler. The Mosaic Covenant, now called the "Old Covenant" by Christians, functioned as the relational and legal structure that gave direction and substance to the nation. It was primarily a *relational* entity—a covenant. It was secondarily a *legal* entity—a constitution, if you will. The tithe (giving 1/10) was a part of Israel's relational and legal commitments to her God and Ruler. As is appropriate with those in earlier stages of faith, God taught His people about generous giving by giving them lots of structure to facilitate their generosity. However, the structure was never the end, but rather the means to the more important truths that undergirded it. These truths are two-sided: one side is seeing God as our Creator and the Gracious Giver of all things. On the other is God's people recognizing His provision and responding in grateful generosity in giving back to Him. All of Israel's giving guidelines could be reduced to these truths.

The tithe in Israel was a relational statement of dependence and gratitude to a covenant-making God. Additionally, the tithe was a "political" statement in that it functioned as a "theocratic tax" that God had also designed to sustain the nation's theocratic structure. Therefore, through their tithing Israelites were expressing both relational and "political" relationships with God. While there were free-will giving options under the Old (Mosaic) Covenant, much of the Old Testament's discussion about giving centers around the covenantal obligation of the tithe *that God's people had committed to sustain* when they entered into the Mosaic Covenant (Exodus 19:7-8).

Fast-forward one thousand years to about 432 B.C. A remnant of Israel is back in the land during the time of the prophet Malachi. He is exhorting them to maintain the tithe as a part of their Old Covenant obligation to the Lord (Malachi 3:7-12). The prophet warns that if they don't, they will experience *the curses* of the Old Covenant in Deuteronomy 28:15-68 that God had told them about a millennium earlier. However, if they would repent and give generously as they had committed to do, God would pour out *the blessings* of the covenant (Deut 28:1-14). God was serious about teaching His children to be generous givers. However, under the Old Covenant, it was highly structured, as is appropriate for underage children, and *three tithes* were mandated in the Mosaic Law.[19] The **first tithe** was 1/10 of all and called "the Lord's tithe" and "the storehouse tithe." It was given to the Levites for their service in the tabernacle/temple (Leviticus 27:30-33; Numbers 18:21-32). The **second tithe** was 1/10 of the remaining 9/10 and was called "the Israelites' tithe." It was set

---

[19] There is no clear consensus among Old Testament scholars about whether there were three different tithes in Israel or whether the three sets of instructions about tithing were to bring out three different facets of the one tithe. To this author it is hard to correlate the three very different foci and emphases of the three sets of instructions with only one tithe. Additionally, given the "theocratic tax" dimension of the tithes, it seems far more likely that 19-22% of each Israelite family's income would be needed to keep the theocratic infrastructure going rather than 10%.

apart and spent on the food and drink of a sacred meal in Jerusalem "in the presence of the Lord your God" (Deut 12:5-19; 14:22-27). Those living too far from Jerusalem to bring animals, grain, wine, and oil could exchange the value of their produce for money to be spent on the meal. The **third tithe** was an additional tithe that was 1/10 of the remaining 8/10 balance every third year. It was a "charity or benevolence tithe" that was for the Levites, aliens, orphans, and widows in one's local community because they have no inheritance in the land (Deut 14:28-29).

The cumulative effect of the three tithes was to encourage generous and holistic giving in three different areas: to those who serve the Lord in His tabernacle or temple, for celebration before the Lord, and for the poor in your area. If there are two tithes, then the total "tithe" = 19% per year. If there are three tithes, then the total "tithe" = approximately 22% per year. God was serious about teaching His children to give generously and "tithing" to an Israelite was not just a 10% thing! The Old Testament models generous giving far more dramatically than we ever imagined.

When our children were young, my wife Marty and I used the "envelope system". We would give them their monthly allowance in bills so that they could divide their money into various envelopes marked "Clothing," "Fun Money," "Birthday Gifts," "Giving to the Lord," etc. The plan was to instill internal, intrinsic motivation for generous giving by starting with external, extrinsic structures to guide them. We used structured patterns when they were young to prepare them for the greater freedom and responsibility of adulthood. Such a plan is not original with us. We learned it by observing how God taught His children Israel as minors before Messiah came and inaugurated the New Covenant age of adulthood. The child-appropriate external structure was to give way to the adult-appropriate internal motivation.

A Summary of Giving in the Old Testament

There are many other things that we could say about the reasons and practices of generous giving in the Old Testament. However, let me simply summarize and develop some things we have only briefly discussed. First, underlying all giving in the Old Testament is recognition of God as Creator and Generous Provider. Ideally, this recognition would engender a loving response of gratitude to God and a rather immediate expression of that love by giving back the tithes to God. The offering of the first-fruits of crops, fruit, animals, etc. captures the timely recognition and expressions of loving gratitude to God. While the instructions about offering these tithes are structured and specific, one cannot help but believe that they were all directed toward Old Covenant believers cultivating a grateful and responsive heart toward God as a way-of-life. The tithes were not ends in and of themselves, but were most likely means to the ultimate end of nurturing a nation full of grateful, God-focused believers.

Secondly, looking at the three tithes in Israel, we can see that God wanted the expressions of gratitude to Him in His people's tithes to finance and facilitate the ongoing spiritual machinery of the nation. This is the "theocratic tax" dimension of the tithes. In other words, God wanted the priests, Levites, tabernacle/temple, and those without inheritance in the land to be cared for out of the tithes of His people. God passed on *His gifts* to those who served Him, to facilitate worship (especially with the second tithe), to care for the places where the people worshipped Him, and to care for those who were hindered in caring for themselves. God's generosity seems to know no ends. Giving back to God was also generously giving to targeted people and causes.

Thirdly, in addition to the structured tithes that were *paid* or *brought* like taxes, there was also the option under the Old Covenant of *giving* "freewill gifts" or "voluntary gifts" which were over and above the tithes and first-fruits (Leviticus 22:17-25; Numbers 15:1-10; Deuteronomy 12:6, 17).[20] An example of giving freewill offerings would be the materials and precious metals that God's people gave for the building of the tabernacle in Exodus 35:20-29:

> "The Israelites, all the men and women, *whose heart moved them to bring material for all the work*, which the Lord had commanded through Moses to be done, *brought a freewill offering to the Lord.*"

Four hundred years later, King David and many of the rulers and leaders of Israel gave generous freewill gifts for the

---

[20] Interestingly enough, during the Old Covenant era when God's people were minors, even the "freewill giving" had guidelines and structures (e.g., Leviticus 22:18-25).

building of the temple:

> "Then the people rejoiced because *they had offered so willingly, for they made their offering to the Lord with a whole heart*, and King David also rejoiced greatly" (1 Chronicles 29:9).[21]

These gifts that usually were given to God could also be given to others, especially to the poor. Proverbs 19:17 ties the two recipients of God and the poor together: "He who is gracious to a poor man lends to the Lord, and He will repay him for his good deed."

All throughout the Old Testament, generosity to the poor (giving "alms") is encouraged and admired. God was clearly delighted that a portion of Israel's giving was to be focused on meeting the needs of the needy, especially through freewill giving.

---

[21] Ironically, about six hundred years later when the temple needed to be rebuilt after the exile, the Israelites again gave freewill offerings for this task (Ezra 1:4-11; 3:4-5; 7:16; 8:24-30).

There are some wonderful things to be learned from Israel's obligatory giving. While it is not still *regulatory* as our giving practice, it is still *revelatory*. We can learn much about *the underlying principles* while we leave *the practices* behind. It is these principles upon which New Covenant giving is built. It is also instructive to see how the whole area of freewill giving has been expanded in the New Testament. That being the case, let's turn to the adult giving practices of God's people in the age of Jesus the Messiah.

Grace-Giving: The New Testament Pattern of Generosity for God's People as Adults

Although many desire to ground the reason for Christian giving under the New Covenant upon the "tithe", this attempt fails to gain the support of the New Testament. While tithing is modeled and discussed by Jesus in the gospels, this is simply because Jesus and His disciples were still functioning under the constraints of the Mosaic Covenant. This Law Covenant was in effect until Jesus inaugurated the New Covenant with His death and resurrection. Therefore, the discussions about tithing in the gospels are simply *descriptive, not prescriptive* for New Covenant believers. Jesus lived under the on-going theocratic state of Israel and obeyed His Father's laws about its functioning. However, the New Testament reveals that Jesus inaugurated a multi-ethnic, international people who are scattered among many nations to replace the theocratic state of Israel. Jesus thereby ended the theocratic tax of tithing for His followers.

The Concept of Grace-Giving

In the place of tithing, there are several other reasons for giving. They all cluster around the central New Testament concept of grace-giving. *"Grace giving" is choosing to give according to the resources God has given you.* 2 Corinthians 8-9 is the longest and most complete discussion of grace-giving in the New Testament. Here are three verses from this central passage that set forth this New Covenant pattern of giving:

"For I testify that *according to their ability*, and beyond their ability *they gave of their own accord*"(2 Cor 8:3).

"For if the readiness is present, *it is acceptable according to what a person has, not according to what he does not have*" (2 Cor 8:12).

"*Let each one do just as he has purposed in his heart*; not grudgingly or under compulsion; for God loves a cheerful giver" (2 Cor 9:7).

This pattern of choosing to give as God has blessed you is also modeled by the young church in Antioch of Syria in the Book of Acts:

"And *in the proportion that any of the disciples had means, each of them determined* to send a contribution for the relief of the brethren living in Judea" (Acts 11:29).

As the language of the New Testament makes clear, grace-giving is a continuation of the freewill or voluntary giving of the Old Covenant. What was *the optional pattern* of giving under the Old Covenant is now *the normal pattern* of giving under the New. In this we see that the highly structured paying of tithes as a theocratic tax is now replaced by believers choosing to give in their own heart according to their own means. The "fullness of time" that Jesus has inaugurated has brought with it the shift from childlike external structure to adult-like internal motivation in giving.

Therefore, the answer to our question, "Is generous giving defined by a percentage?" is that it is *not* under the New Covenant. However, if the Old Testament is instructive in the matter, we should at least be as generous under the New Covenant as God encouraged His people to be under the Old. Should one set giving of 10% as a baseline for giving? Perhaps. But if the Old Covenant percentage was actually

19-22%, then such a baseline would need to be rethought. The bigger problem is that we are really comparing apples and oranges when we compare giving in the theocratic state of Israel with giving under the New Covenant. If the tithe in Israel is viewed as a theocratic tax, then it corresponds to our modern pattern of paying taxes to state and federal governments. This means that the only correspondence left would then be between the Old Covenant's freewill giving and the New Covenant's grace-giving. If this is the case, then we do not have any fixed percentages to go by. Rather, we must rely on the patterns and motivations of both the Old and New Covenants that encourage generous giving. With such adult-like freedom comes adult-like responsibility. This is why we must do a significantly better job of teaching people in the area of giving. Biblical teaching and biblical motivations to give become immensely important with the New Covenant freedom of grace-giving.

So, *how* should we give? The following

chapter seeks to unpack the multifaceted expressions of grace-giving.

WHAT DOES GENEROUS GIVING LOOK LIKE UNDER THE NEW COVENANT?

The New Testament spells out two areas in which believers are responsible to choose to give. While this giving shares the obligatory nature of the Old Covenant tithe, it does not share the prescribed amount or a prescribed regularity for the giving. Rather, the Scriptures just say that Christians are "bound" or "indebted" to choose to give in these areas.

Believers Should Give to Those Who Give Them Spiritual Things

This is an area that continues the Old Covenant principle of giving where God's people gave to Him by giving to the priests and Levites who ministered before them. The New Testament repeats the principle to give to those who minister to us; encouraging us that when others minister spiritual things to us, we are indebted to minister to them with material things (Romans 15:27). Paul articulates this principle in different forms in various passages:

"If we sowed spiritual things in you, is it too much if we should reap material things from you?" (1 Cor 9:11).

"So also the Lord directed those who proclaim the gospel to get their living from the gospel" (1 Cor 9:14).

"And let the one who is taught the Word share all good things with him who teaches" (Galatians 6:6).

"Let the elders who rule well be

considered worthy of double honor, especially those who work hard at preaching and teaching. For the Scripture says, 'You shall not muzzle the ox while he is threshing,' and 'The laborer is worthy of his wages'" (1 Tim 5:17-18).[22]

Note the principle for giving financially to those who give to you spiritually is one of "indebtedness" or very real obligation. This kind of reciprocal spiritual and financial ministry is how God has always cared for those who serve Him as a way-of-life. Particularly, we see that while it is something that New Covenant believers ought to do, it is nonetheless also a voluntary thing we should choose to do. At stake is the loving care of those who have given their lives and "careers" for the sake of the gospel. Of all people these dear saints should be well cared for financially.

The principle of ministering financially

---

[22] Note "honor" also has a financial connotation in 1 Timothy 5:3, 8

to those who have ministered to us spiritually is obviously applicable to the leaders who serve us within our local church. This is why giving to our local congregation is not an optional thing biblically, but rather is an appropriate obligation in fulfilling our reciprocal ministry to those who give us spiritual things. Before the Lord we have an "indebtedness" that we should honorably fulfill. This is one of the beautiful choices and responsibilities of spiritual adulthood under the New Covenant.

I had an interesting experience recently after teaching this principle in a class in a local church. The next week one of the members of the class shared that she was impressed by the Lord to recognize her responsibility to minister financially to the Christian college from which she had graduated a few years before. It was a new thought to her, but she had begun to recognize that her school had ministered many spiritual things to her and that she had the responsibility to minister back to her alma mater financially. This application probably holds true for all parachurch ministries. While these Christian organizations are not local churches, they are still one of the main sources of the ministering of spiritual things to us in our culture. Therefore, they also should be the recipients of our reciprocal financial ministry.

Believers Should Give to their Needy Fellow Believers

A part of living under the spiritual adulthood of the New Covenant is being aware of the needs of other believers around us. As we see these needs, we should respond in some financial fashion as we have resources. Paul understands this mutual sharing of resources as so foundational to the life in Christ that he states it as part of the purpose for a Christian working:

"Let him who steals steal no longer; but rather let him labor, performing

with his own hands what is good, in order that he may have something to share with him who has need"
(Ephesians 4:28).

Several other New Testament passages teach and model this principle, but the passages in 1 John are the most pointed and vivid in their expression:

"We know love by this, that He laid down His life for us; and we ought to lay down our lives for the brethren. But whoever has the world's goods, and beholds his brother in need and closes his heart against him, how does the love of God abide in him? Little children, let us not love with word or with tongue, but in deed and truth" (1 John 3:16-18; cf. James 2:14-17).

When the knowledge of spiritual things does not lead to loving Christian expressions of such knowledge, it is neither biblical thinking nor biblical living. The letter of 1 John corrects this kind of false teaching. A part of assuming our responsible role as a sister or brother in God's family is caring for the needs of other members of our family in Christ. The Bible generally defines such "needs" as food, shelter, and clothing. It is these basic necessities of life that we should make sure that every believer around us has met.[23]

While the application of this principle of sharing our financial resources with needy fellow believers immediately around us is fairly obvious, what is not so obvious is our responsibility to fellow Christians who are in other areas or other countries. As we are aware of their needs, should we be sharing from our little pile of the world's goods to meet their needs? In an age of astonishing amounts of information about people around the world, this can quickly be overwhelming. What should we

---

[23] For a brilliant (and convicting!) summary of the early church's views of sharing with one another, see Justo L. González, *Faith & Wealth: A History of Early Christian Ideas on the Origin, Significance, and Use of Money* (San Francisco, CA: Harper & Row Publishers, 1990).

do?

Perhaps a couple of points may prove suggestive regarding this issue. First, remember that New Covenant giving is grace giving—choosing to give according to the resources God has given us. If we want to choose to give to needy believers (and non-believers) in other areas and other parts of the world, this is a wonderful and admirable choice. God will bless our giving. However, it is probably not as central a focus in giving as other areas are. We should make sure that we cover the priority areas first. The plethora of these areas will be obvious by the end of this book.

Secondly, the New Testament seems to focus on sharing resources with needy believers in other areas at the church-to-church level. At this level we should be very aware of the needs beyond those of our own local congregation. There are also certain principles and obligations that apply in the area of church-to-church giving. This is a very neglected area of study when we discuss New Covenant giving. Because of this we need to spend some time unpacking what the New Testament says about it.

Church-to-Church Giving

The longest discussion of giving in the Bible, 2 Corinthians 8-9, is intended to motivate a local church to follow through on its pledge to give to churches in another part of the world. In other words, Paul was exhorting the exuberant and immature Corinthian church to give to the collection for the poor saints in the Jerusalem and Judea area. He was challenging Greek Christians, most of whom were Gentiles, to finish the international collection for Jewish Christians that the Corinthians had started over a year earlier.[24] Paul had given them specific instructions about how to finish this collection in his previous letter:

"Now concerning the collection for the saints, as I directed the churches of Galatia, so do you also. On the first day of every week let each of you put aside and save, as he may prosper, that no collections be made when I come. And when I arrive, whomever you may approve, I shall send them with letters to carry your gift to Jerusalem; and if it is fitting for me to go also, they will go

---

[24] If a person wants to understand giving in the New Testament, I cannot emphasize enough that 2 Corinthians 8-9 is the place to begin and spend a very significant amount of time. Because it is the longest discussion of giving in the Bible, it is worthy of being the starting point for our study and our discussions. For a very helpful and accessible discussion of giving in these chapters, see Craig L. Blomberg, *Neither Poverty nor Riches: A Biblical Theology of Possessions* (Leicester: InterVarsity Press; Grand Rapids, MI: Eerdmans, 1999; Downers Grove, IL: InterVarsity Press, 2001) 190-199.

with me" (1 Cor 16:1-4).[25]

However, Paul was now concerned that they would not have completed the collection when he arrived from Macedonia (northern Greece) and he and they would be put to shame (2 Corinthians 9:1-4). Thus, Paul was writing and sending Titus to avoid such an embarrassment (2 Corinthians 8:16-24) and the New Testament practice of church-to-church giving was explained in some detail. Moreover, Paul continues this discussion and collection in the next letter

---

[25] Note the very practical advice for each Christian of setting aside some money each Sunday for the collection according to how God had blessed him or her ("as he may prosper" in v. 2). Note also the instructions about choosing a representative from the church to accompany the completed collection. The other contributing churches had already done this. Acts 20:3-4 recounts Paul's arrival in Corinth a few months later and lists these church's representatives. These representatives would not only personalize this large collection on behalf of their churches in Jerusalem, but they would also protect all these coins on the way to Jerusalem!

he writes: to the house churches in Rome. [26] In Romans Paul also explains the international collection for the poor Judean believers and begins to motivate the Roman church to contribute to it also (Romans 1:11-13; 15:22-29).[27]

---

[26] For the broader New Testament backdrop for Paul's raising of this money, see Jouette M. Bassler, *God & Mammon: Asking for Money in the New Testament* (Nashville, TN: Abingdon Press, 1991), especially 89-115. For "a brief history of Christian fundraising," see Chapter 3 with that title in Thomas H. Jeavons and Rebekah Burch Basinger, *Growing Givers' Hearts: Treating Fundraising as Ministry* (San Francisco, CA: Jossey-Bass, 2000) 55-67.

[27] In Romans 1:13b Paul says that often he had planned to come to Rome "in order that I might obtain some fruit among you also, even as among the rest of the Gentiles." Some translations like the NIV translate fruit (Greek, *karpos*) as an evangelistic harvest. However, Paul's usage of fruit in Romans 15:28 (a parallel passage at the end of the letter when he explains his intentions more fully) shows that the term refers to the collection for the Judean churches. This collection continued to be very much on his mind in the weeks and months after he wrote 2 Corinthians 8-9. See especially, M. A. Kruger, "Tina Karpon, 'Some Fruit' in Romans 1:13," *Westminster Theological Journal* 49 (1987) 167-173.

Churches Should Fulfill the Principle of Material Gifts for Spiritual Benefits

It is very interesting that the principle we encountered earlier about sharing material things with those who give you spiritual things also applies to churches who received such things from other churches:

> For Macedonia and Achaia have been pleased to make a contribution for the poor among the saints in Jerusalem. Yes, they were pleased to do so, and they are indebted to them. For if the Gentiles have shared in their spiritual things, they are indebted to minister to them also in material things (Romans 15:26-27).

Noting Paul's rationale is very important here. He had been teaching for some time to other churches, and now is including the Romans in the loop, that all of the Gentile Christians of the eastern Roman

Empire were given spiritual things, i.e., the gospel, by the first believers, the Jewish Christians of Jerusalem and Judea. Now, these Gentile Christian churches are "indebted" to give back financially to the Jewish Christian churches in and around Jerusalem. These churches are impoverished due to persecution, famine, and radical financial sacrifices early in the Church's history (Acts 4:32-37). It is time to honor their earlier spiritual ministry to the Gentiles with a reciprocal financial ministry. This is also one reason why Paul wrote 2 Corinthians 8-9: to honor the biblical principle of spiritual and financial reciprocity on a church-to-church basis.

A few weeks ago I heard about a very large, well-known suburban church in Southern California that was celebrating its fifty-year anniversary. To commemorate this milestone, this large church gave a gift of $100,000 to a small, struggling inner city church in Los Angeles. What motivated their gift? It was the principle of one church giving back financially to another church that had ministered to them spiritually. The inner city church had been one of the first churches of this particular denomination in Southern California. Over its long history, it had been a generous source of its denomination's church-planting in the area. Several churches owed their existence to this small Los Angeles church, including the suburban megachurch. However, now the old, inner city church was struggling financially. What a wonderful time to honor her long history of giving away spiritual things by reciprocating with material things! What a wonderful time to fulfill the "indebtedness" of honoring spiritual ministry with material ministry through church-to-church giving. This family-of-God-reciprocity is another beautiful facet of the biblical pattern of grace-giving for

God's adult, New Covenant people.[28]

Churches Should Fulfill
the Principle of Maintaining Equality
Among Churches

Another motivation for church-to-church giving has to do with making sure basic needs are being met among the various churches. What is astonishing about Paul's application of this principle in 2 Corinthians 8 is that he applies it on an international basis!

---

[28] For a very helpful explanation of the obligation of "generalized reciprocity" among brothers and sisters in the first century Mediterranean world, see the important book by my dear friend and Biola University colleague, Joseph H. Hellerman, *The Ancient Church as Family* (Minneapolis, MN: Fortress Press, 2001) 47-51. Joe demonstrates how Paul appeals to this concept in 2 Corinthians 8-9 (pp. 110-113). "Generalized reciprocity" is the relationship between brothers and sisters that "shares resources without specification of some return obligation in terms of time, quantity, or quality" (p. 47). By Jesus and the apostles using the terminology of "sisters and brothers" to describe relationships within the Church, the dynamic of reciprocity of material resources is assumed.

In other words he is seeking to establish some equality in the meeting of basic needs among the churches on a global basis. Again, this involves the contributing of the Gentile churches of the eastern Mediterranean world to the Jewish Christian churches of the Jerusalem area:

> "For if the readiness is present, it is acceptable according to what a man has, not according to what he does not have. For this is not for the ease of others and for your affliction, but by way of equality—at this present time your abundance being a supply for their want, that their abundance also may become a supply for your want, that there may be equality; as it is written, 'He who gathered much did not have too much, and he who gathered little had no lack'" (2 Cor 8:12-15).[29]

---

[29] "The ideal state of affairs is an equality achieved by free giving and receiving, by a sharing in common, not by all goods becoming public property, publicly administered." Ben Witherington, *Conflict & Community in Corinth*, 421.

It is difficult at present to imagine that the wealthy churches of the West could ever be in financial need necessitating the monetary help of our brothers and sisters in the Asian, Latin American, and African churches. However, it is not unlikely that such a day may come. It has already come spiritually. The majority of Christians are now in the southern hemisphere.[30] Additionally, the greatest spiritual vibrancy of the Church worldwide is now found in Africa, Latin America, and Asia. These churches are already supplying the vast majority of the next wave of missionaries as the missionary numbers from Europe and North America continue to dwindle. Additionally, spiritual leadership is already being supplied by the two-thirds world in maintaining biblical grounding in various denominations in the face of growing theological liberalism in

---

[30] For the statistics to support this and what follows, see Justin Long and Jason Mandryk, "The State of the Gospel," Momentum (November/December, 2006) 22-79. See also www.momentum-mag.org.

the West. Moreover, a little-known fact is that the largest churches in Europe are now pastored by Africans! There is an astonishing spiritual equality that has emerged on a global basis.

However, there is still the need for the Church in the West to be sensitive to the need for equality in meeting basic physical and spiritual necessities on a global basis. While we continue to gather extra, we should be aware of and contributing to the needs of our sisters and brothers in Christ around the world who are not able to gather enough to meet their basic physical needs and to care adequately for God's people. These include not only the physical necessities of food, shelter, and clothing, but also the spiritual necessities of the Bible in their own language, biblical training materials in their own language and within their own worldview, and adequate training for their pastors and Christian leaders. I haven't even touched on adequate places where God's people could meet in relative safety and minimal comfort.

It is these kinds of needs that church-to-church giving can meet. It is these kinds of needs that Paul spent years of his missionary life meeting! While he did plant churches and teach and train believers, he also spent countless days teaching, motivating, and exhorting the churches of the eastern Mediterranean area to be involved in maintaining some sense of global equality among the churches of Jesus Christ. Can we say the same about our sensitivities and priorities?

Missionary Giving
by Individuals and Churches

Another facet of grace-giving under the New Covenant is the investment in the spreading of the gospel beyond one's local church. This grace-giving by individuals and churches is in addition to reciprocating with financial gifts for spiritual benefits and maintaining some sense of equality by meeting the needs of fellow believers and sister churches. The term used in the New Testament for this type of giving is *koinōnia* or "sharing, partnership". *Koinōnia* is also the Greek word translated "fellowship" and it generally ends up as the title of church fellowship halls, Sunday School classes, Bible study groups, etc. However, in Philippians 1:3-5 Paul speaks of the Philippian church's investment in his ministry as a missionary in terms of their *koinōnia* or sharing and partnering with him in the gospel cause. This is a fairly typical usage of *koinōnia* relating to business or investment partnerships:

> "I thank my God in all my remembrance of you, always in every prayer of mine for you all making my prayer with joy, because of *your partnership in the gospel* from the first day until now" (ESV).

At the end of this letter, in Philippians 4:10-20, Paul resumes this talk of financial partnership and gives his "thank you" for their support of him. Apparently, no other church had the foresight to have *koinōnia* in Paul's ministry except the Philippians (Philippians 4:14-15, where a form of *koinōnia* is used twice). They had sent a gift for his needs more than once (4:16). What a lost opportunity of tragic proportions for other believers and other churches! Think of the spiritual fruit that resulted from investing in the Apostle Paul's ministry. He wrote:

> "Not that I seek the gift itself, but I seek for the *profit* (lit. *fruit) which increases to your account*" (Philippians 4:17).[31]

---

[31] Philippians 1:6 is also an encouragement about the Philippians' financial partnering with Paul in the gospel cause (1:3-5). In its context, the "good work" in 1:6 is this partnering or *koinōnia* by the Philippians, which shall come to full fruition at the return of Christ. This is the language of a financial investment coming to full maturity. See Gerald F. Hawthorne, *Word Biblical Commentary: Philippians*, Revised and Expanded by Ralph P. Martin (Vol. 43; Nashville, TN: Thomas Nelson Publishers, 2004) on Philippians 1:6 for a fuller discussion of this interpretation. The only better financial partnering in all of human history would have been sharing in the financing of Jesus' ministry with the women mentioned in Luke 8:1-3!

One wonders if this small percentage of churches in Paul's day that understood the importance of investing in the advance of the gospel cause is typical of the lack of giving perspective of many churches throughout history.

Several years ago I was a pastor and was confronted with the financial challenges of planting and growing a church along with my fellow elders. In light of the teaching of Philippians, one of our fundamental commitments was the priority of investing in the advance of the gospel cause beyond our own local church. Early in the life of the church, we committed to have *koinōnia* with other ministries beyond our borders. We committed to invest 30% of every dollar that was given to us for the broader advance of the gospel. Every six months we wanted to increase this percentage by 5% until we got to 50%.

Our idealism was soon tested when our church treasurer said that we could either pay the staff salaries in two weeks or pay our financial commitments to our missionaries and mission organizations. Suddenly, this *koinōnia* thing became very personal! My wife and I had two young children and absolutely no financial buffer at the time. Missing a paycheck would be devastating to us as a family. However, as the other elders and I meditated on Paul's words about investing in the gospel cause in Philippians 4:10-20, we took heart. The Lord knew that local churches like us would regularly feel the conflict between investing in their local needs and investing in the broader gospel advance. This is why the Lord stirred Paul to include the promise to local churches in Philippians 4:19: "And my God shall supply all your needs according to His riches in glory in Christ Jesus." As a group of elders, we claimed this promise (some of us more vigorously than others!) and went ahead and made our missions' investments. Sure enough, the Lord met our local needs and we were able to pay our staff salaries in the next two weeks.[32]

By continuing to give priority to our investment in the broader advance of the gospel, we were always able to meet our local needs in the seven years I was at the church. God was astonishingly faithful to supply all our needs as He promised in His Word. Moreover, we had the unspeakable joy of investing in what God was doing in many parts of the world. One of the anticipated joys of being with the Lord in the future is looking forward to seeing the full maturity of our investment in the day of Christ Jesus (Philippians 1:6).

---

[32] See Peter T. O'Brien, *New International Greek Testament Commentary: Philippians* (Grand Rapids, MI: William B. Eerdmans Publishing Company, 1991) 543-549 for a thorough discussion of this promise in Philippians 4:19.

CONCLUSION

We have covered much ground in this book on the biblical perspective on giving. We have answered the question, "Why does God want us to give generously?" with the Bible's answer: our giving will radically change us and others both now and for eternity. For this astonishing change to occur, we looked at the question, "Is generous giving defined by a percentage?" The Scripture's answer is that it was defined from a minimum of 10% to a maximum of over 22% during the theocratic kingdom era of the Old Covenant. But, with the inauguration of the New Covenant by Jesus and the ending of the previous theocracy, God's people are now scattered among all the nations. Now we pay taxes to our respective governments and do grace-giving to the Lord that's not defined according to any percentage. If we want to use the Old Covenant tithe as a baseline, remember that we may be looking at over 22%. I don't think this is the standard that most folks intend! Therefore, we're on much surer ground to educate and emphasize generous grace-giving with the Bible's non-percentage motivations.

So, "What does generous New Covenant giving look like?" It begins by giving to those who minister to us as well as to needy believers. Then our giving for church-to-church giving and to maintain international equality (to advance the gospel cause) quickly deflates a figure like 10%. Personally, I think that we should give much more than 1/10. However, my opinion is just that and we would do much better to focus on what the New Testament emphasizes:

"Let each one do just as he has purposed in his heart; not grudgingly or under compulsion; for God loves a cheerful giver" (2 Cor 9:7).

With such freedom of choice regarding generous giving comes great responsibility. Generous love breeds generous freedom. May God help us to respond to His overwhelming generosity with a generosity of our own.

ABOUT THE AUTHOR

Dr. Walt Russell studied what the Bible teaches about giving while earning three graduate theological degrees. Along the way he's lived out these principles as a missionary, businessman, church planter, and pastor. He has been teaching these truths in his New Testament and biblical interpretation classes at Biola University's Talbot School of Theology since 1990. He is a popular speaker who delights in equipping other to be spiritually formed by God's Word and is the author of *Playing with Fire: How the Bible Ignites Change in Your Soul* (NavPress, 2000).

NOTES

NOTES

NOTES

NOTES